Table of Contents

Introduction. vii
Chapter 1 - Born Again 1
Chapter 2 - Love and Justice. 5
Chapter 3 - The Battle Within 11
Chapter 4 - Enemy Territory 21
Chapter 5 - Not of this World. 29
Chapter 6 - Who Do You Love? 37
Chapter 7 - Sons of the Devil 45
Chapter 8 - The Great Commission 55
Chapter 9 - True Worship 63
Chapter 10 - Are You? 73

Introduction

A great sadness fills my heart when I look at Christianity today. Holy Scripture is clear on what it means to be Christian, but it seems that many have lost their way. Over two billion people in this world claim to be Christian and yet how many of these people are following the Biblical pattern for what it means to be a child of God? Some churches have fallen into the routine of ritual and ceremony. Some have strayed from the path of Biblical truth and allowed the values of the unsaved world to seep in, while others have even rejected the truth of Scripture. False teachers are spreading false gospels, leading people to believe that they are saved, when in fact they are not. And so it goes on.

There is only one place to go to find the truth of what it really means to be Christian and that place is the Bible, the word of God. That's why I wrote this book. If you believe that you are a Christian, the only way to be assured of your faith is by studying the Bible. When you compare yourself to what is revealed in holy Scripture, you will discover the truth of your salvation. My hope is that this book will be a starting point for you to test yourself and see if you pass or fail that test. Are you truly a Christian? Are you truly born again? Let's find out.

Born Again

Truly, truly, I say to you, unless one is born again he cannot see the kingdom of God. (John 3:3)

With every tick of the clock we get closer and closer to the end of this age. The final seven years will be a time of great tribulation when God pours out His wrath upon the world in judgement. This will culminate in the return of the Lord Jesus Christ. He will chain up the devil and rule on earth for a thousand years, with Jerusalem as the seat of His kingdom. At the end of that thousand years the devil will be released and will lead a revolt against the Son of God. Satan will deceive many into forming an army that will surround Jerusalem, but this revolt will be quickly extinguished, as fire will rain down from heaven to destroy all those who challenge the Lord. The devil will then be thrown into the lake of fire and the entire universe will be destroyed. Then comes the judgement. Christians; those who put their faith in Jesus Christ, will spend all eternity in the very presence of God the Almighty and His Son.

So what does it mean to be Christian? More than two billion people in this world claim to be Christian. They believe themselves to be saved and on their way to heaven, but are they?

In His conversation with a religious leader named Nicodemus, our Lord Jesus said *"unless one is **born again**, he cannot see the kingdom of God."* (John 3:3) The Greek word for 'again' is 'anōthen' and is often translated *'from above.'* For instance, when John the Baptist says *"He who comes from above is above all"* (John 3:31) that same word 'anōthen' is used. In the case of Jesus speaking to Nicodemus I feel both translations are accurate. We are born again to new life, spiritual life, and the source of this new birth is God who reigns from above.

The Apostle Paul tells us *"if anyone is in Christ, he is **a new creature**; the old things passed away; behold, new things have come."* (2 Corinthians 5:17) If you are born again you are no longer what you were, because you are *"a new creature."* You are no longer spiritually dead, but spiritually alive to God through Jesus Christ. Paul tells us: *"But God, being rich in mercy, because of His great love with which He loved us, even when we were dead in our transgressions, made us alive together with Christ."* (Ephesians 2:4,5)

So what does this new birth look like? How can we be certain that we are truly born again?

The great concern of my heart is that so many people believe themselves to be saved, yet there is no evidence of their salvation. There are people involved in false religious systems who have been deceived by those systems. There are false teachers who present false gospels, thus deceiving the people who follow them by giving their listeners a false sense of security of their salvation. Many churches have become social clubs where they don't teach the word of God, therefore leaving congregations ignorant of what it really means to be Christian. Professing Christians are being seduced by the unbelieving world and their committment to Christ is shallow at best. I long to see people who call themselves Christian to be living in accordance with all that holy Scripture reveals, so they can be assured that their faith is real.

The Apostle Paul gives both warning and advice when he instructs us to *"Test yourselves to see if you are in the faith; examine yourselves! Or do you not recognize this about yourselves, that Jesus Christ is in you - unless indeed you fail the test?"* (2 Corinthians 13:5)

There are many evidences of our new birth and in this book we will go to the source of all truth, the Bible, to see what Scripture reveals about what it really means to be born again. I pray that you will test yourselves and be encouraged and strengthened by the reality of your faith. And for those who fail the test, I pray that you will embrace the truth of the gospel and sincerely be born again.

Love and Justice

The time is fulfilled, and the kingdom of God is at hand; repent and believe in the gospel.
(Mark 1:15)

To help understand what it truly means to be born again, the right place to start is with the gospel. Without the gospel there is no Christianity. Without the true gospel, there are no true Christians.

So many people in this world are confused as to how we gain entry into the kingdom of God. Some believe that we work our way into heaven. Others believe that if we do more good deeds than bad, then we will avoid eternal damnation. To make things even more confusing there are many false teachers proclaiming all sorts of false gospels. Some promote God as a sort of spiritual Santa Claus who wants to make you wealthy and bless you with material possessions. Others say Jesus will fix your problems and make your life better. A famous pastor from a very large church says he believes people who are not Christian will go to heaven because they are good people. Is that the gospel? No, not even close.

Every human being who ever lived, apart from Jesus Christ, is a sinner. This is why we all commit sins. What is sin? The essence of sin is disobedience which originates from pride. God gave Adam one rule to obey and he disobeyed that rule. Adam brought sin into the world and into human nature. As Adam is the father of us all, we all inherited that nature. Think about it, we don't have to teach our children to be disobedient or selfish, do we? It comes naturally.

It's in our natural human nature to break God's rules, or laws. Therefore a sinner is a lawbreaker and lawbreakers are punished, just like in human society.

The punishment for sin is to be eternally separated from God in a place of never ending torment. This is the place we commonly call hell. Every single moment in hell will be one of misery, anguish, rage and regret. Justice demands that we all be sent to hell, because we all sin and yet God loved us so much that He made a way for us to avoid the punishment we so rightfully deserve.

God sent His Son Jesus Christ into the world. The Holy Spirit came upon Mary and the virgin girl became pregnant. Therefore the child in her womb would be the Son of Man (mankind) and the Son of God; both human and God.

Jesus lived a sinless life and was crucified on a Roman cross. On the third day after His crucifixion He came back to life, thus proving that He truly is the Son of God and death could not hold Him.

Jesus went to the cross and took the punishment for the sins of the world upon Himself, so that those who believe in Him will have their sins forgiven and hell is not their eternal destination.

If we put our faith in God through Jesus Christ we will be given the gift of eternal life. God will place His Holy Spirit within us to help and teach us. We will spend all eternity with God and His beloved Son in a place where there is no sadness, no pain and no death. This is the gospel.

The evil of sin goes much deeper than simply breaking God's laws. Sin is rebellion against God. Sinners don't accept God for who He is; Creator and sovereign ruler of all that exists. As sinners we refuse God's rule over us and we attempt to rule ourselves. God is no longer worshiped or obeyed as He is worthy and we replace Him with ourselves. We all want to be our own gods, so to speak. We reject God's authority over us in defiance of our Creator. We foolishly believe that we can live by our own rules, but we are all part of God's creation and the reality is that we are still under His authority. God's perfect righteousness and justice demands punishment for sin. Yet God loved us so much that He sent His beloved Son to pay the penalty for the sins of all who put their faith in Him. It is only through Jesus Christ that we can be saved. Scripture tells us *"there is salvation in no one else; for there is no other name under heaven that has been given among men by which we must be saved."* (Acts 4:12)

Many years ago I heard a story about a tribal chief and an amazing event that happened in his village. At one time in the tribe's history it was discovered that someone was stealing. Only small trinkets were stolen, but a thief in the midst of the village was damaging to the tribe. Stealing was not tolerated.

The chief gathered the tribe and called for the thief to step forward. He announced that they would stand there day and night until the thief revealed himself. The only honorable thing to do was to own up to his crime. Everyone knew that the punishment for stealing was forty lashes with the whip.

Eventually the crowd parted and a little old lady revealed herself as the thief. The chief was devastated. The little old lady was his own dear sweet mother.

The tribe stood in silence to see what the chief would do. Would he forsake justice and let his mother go without punishment, showing favoritism and thus weakness? Or would he allow his mother to endure the full penalty for the crime, knowing that she would never survive, therefore killing his own mother?

With steely eyes the chief announced "Tie her to the whipping post!"

Some in the crowd were pleased that the chief showed strength and others were disappointed that he showed no mercy. Just as the whip was raised for the first strike, the chief yelled "Wait!" All eyes turned to the chief as he stepped off his judgement seat and walked towards his frail, old mother. He removed his shirt and wrapped himself around her. Then he announced "You may continue with the punishment."

The chief took all forty lashes upon himself, saving his mother from certain death and yet upholding the laws of his village.

Love for his mother and the strength to uphold justice ruled his decision. The entire village was in awe.

Now think about Jesus Christ. He left the glory of heaven and came to earth for our benefit. The sinless Son of God took the punishment for our sins. The innocent took the punishment for the guilty. He took the wrath of God upon Himself so that we could be offered the gift of salvation. God's justice was upheld and His love for humanity was put on display. Love and justice were harmonized through Jesus Christ. This is the grace and mercy of God; showing kindness to us when we do not deserve this kindness. This is the true gospel.

The gospel is not about Jesus fixing our problems or making us wealthy. It is not about God granting us our sinful desires. It is about saving us from the punishment we deserve. It is about new life; taking us from being spiritually dead to being spiritually alive. The gospel is not something you add to your sinful life because you feel there is something missing. It is dying to your old sinful life and replacing it with new life in Christ. The true gospel is about turning **from sin to God** through faith in Jesus Christ. It is about the gift of eternal life and entrance into the kingdom of God. A kingdom which Jesus says *"is not of this world."* (John 18:36) Therefore this world is not our eternal home and we are no longer the same as the people of this world. We are different, completely different.

Are you attending a church where they don't preach the true gospel? Perhaps you have never even heard the true gospel? If so, then I urge you to repent from your sins and put your faith in the Lord Jesus Christ. When you do an amazing thing happens. You will be transformed from death to life, from the kingdom of darkness to the kingdom of God, all because of the incredible love, mercy and grace of our heavenly Father. You will be born again.

The Battle Within

Wash me thoroughly from my iniquity and cleanse me from my sin. For I know my transgressions, and my sin is ever before me.
(Psalm 51:2,3)

One of the things that makes Christians completely different from the unbelieving world around us is our relationship to sin. Thanks to the sacrifice of the Lord Jesus, Christians have been freed from the penalty of sin and it's control over us. The day will come when we will shed this human body and be free from the sin that remains in us. Until then every Christian battles with sin. No exceptions. This battle is unique to Christians. Unsaved people do not battle with sin, they embrace it. They are willing slaves of sin because they don't know anything else. Yet even for Christians sin is hard to resist, because it still resides in our natural human nature, or as the Bible calls it, our flesh. We fight this internal fight every single day and it is extremely difficult to fight with our own human nature. The born again spirit wants to obey God, whereas our flesh wants to obey sin.

Some believe that being a Christian is as simple as making a one time decision. Praying a prayer or walking down an aisle and then living as if nothing has changed. This is untrue. Being a Christian is a matter of believing all that Scripture reveals. It is about dedicating our entire lives to the glory of God. This involves dying to our sinful selves and living in obedience to Christ. It's not an easy life, because we still inhabit our sinful flesh, but to be born again means that a transformation has occurred.

The Apostle Paul describes this transformation: *"And you were dead in your trespasses and sins, in which you formerly walked according to the course of this world, according to the prince of the power of the air, of the spirit that is now working in the sons of disobedience. Among them we too all formerly lived in the lusts of our flesh, indulging the desires of the flesh and of the mind, and were by nature children of wrath, even as the rest."* (Ephesians 2:1-3)

Notice the Apostle Paul says we *"formerly walked"* as the world does, indicating that if we still behave like unbelievers, then we might not have been transformed at all. If we are not obeying God we may still be *"sons of disobedience."* We might not be born again. We must ask ourselves 'Are we disobeying God and obeying sin?' The Lord Jesus informs us: *"Truly, truly, I say to you, everyone who commits sin is the slave of sin."* (John 8:34) The Apostle Paul confirms this: *"Do you not know that when you present yourselves to someone as slaves for obedience, you are slaves of the one whom you obey, either of sin resulting in death, or of obedience resulting in righteousness?"* (Romans 6:16)

The evil of sin can never be understated. It was sin that brought the fall of mankind which separated us from

Holy God. It was because of sin that the Lord Jesus came to earth and was crucified on a Roman cross, taking the punishment for our sins upon Himself. It was only because of His sacrifice that we could be given the precious gift of salvation. Yet how many people who call themselves Christian take sin seriously? We tend to take God's holy standard of righteousness and compromise by attempting to bring that standard down to a level that makes us feel comfortable. We compare ourselves to other people rather than God's holy law. Yet as Christians, we are to strive for perfection, we strive to be like Christ and live in total obedience to the Father's will.

No-one says it better than the Apostle Paul: *"What shall we say then? Are we to continue in sin so that grace may increase? May it never be! How shall we who died to sin still live in it? Or do you not know that all of us who have been baptized into Christ Jesus have been baptized into His death? Therefore we have been buried with Him through baptism into death, so that as Christ was raised from the dead through the glory of the Father, so we too might walk in newness of life. For if we have become united with Him in the likeness of His death, certainly we shall also be in the likeness of His resurrection, knowing this, that our old self was crucified with Him, in order that our body of sin might be done away with, so that we would no longer be slaves to sin; for he who has died is freed from sin."* (Romans 6:1-7)

I once saw an interview with a pastor from a well known church. During the conversation the interviewer asked "I've been told that you have two homosexual guys singing in your choir. Is that true?" To which the pastor replied "We don't ask people their sexuality when they join the choir. We're not that kind of church. We'll never be that kind of church." To hear this was so disappointing, because Scripture is perfectly clear that *"homosexuals do not inherit eternal life"* (1 Corinthians 6:9,10) How shameful of that pastor not to confront sin in his congregation. How tragic that those two guys are singing in the choir, believing themselves to be Christians on their way to heaven, when in fact they are not. They are not obeying the commands of Scripture to repent. They are not obeying Jesus Christ. Sin is still their master.

In Matthew 7 Jesus is teaching about Judgement Day. He says *"And on that day many will say to me "Lord, Lord, did we not prophesy in Your name and in Your name cast out demons and in Your name perform many miracles?"* Did you notice the word **many** there? This shows that many people who believe themselves to be saved are not. Consider the amazing things these people were doing in the name of Christ. We would think that these people would be truly saved, yet this is not the case. Jesus responds with one of the most frightening things He ever said: *"Then I will declare to them 'I never knew you, depart from Me you who practice lawlessness."* This is a terrifying reality to those who assume to be doing their Master's bidding when in fact they are not. As the Bible teaches us; *"sin is lawlessness."* We have to understand that it doesn't matter what we **'do'** for Christ. If sin is still what we practice, then we are only fooling ourselves. We are not born again and eternal life is not ours. The wrath of God remains on us.

I've heard professing Christians say that they're not too concerned with the Bible, they just 'love Jesus.' But do they? How do we show love for our Lord? Jesus Himself answers: *"If you love me, you will keep my commandments."* (John 14:15) We show love for Christ by our obedience to Him. The Apostle John informs us: *"He who believes in the Son has eternal life; but he who does not **obey** the Son will not see life, but the wrath of God abides on him."* (John 3:36) Obedience is the mark of someone who is truly born again. Yet how can we be obedient if we don't study Scripture? The Bible is the only place that reveals what our Lord requires of us.

Obedience shows faith and trust in God. Our Lord tells us *"whoever does not receive the kingdom of God like a child will not enter it at all."* (Mark 10:15) Think about little children. Who do they trust above everyone else? Their parents. Who supplies all their needs? Their parents. So how do these little ones show love for their parents? In the only way they can; by obedience to them. Parents give their children rules to obey because they only want the best for them. Children show love for their parents by obeying those rules. The same goes for Christians. Everything we have was given to us by God. What can we possibly give to God when everything we have is from Him? So how do we show our love for Him? Just like little children; by our obedience. Also, just like our earthly parents, all our heavenly Father wants for us is good. When we show love to God by our obedience we are blessed. The Apostle Paul tells us *"God causes all things to work together for good to those who **love** God."* (Romans 8:28)

Just like little children, we show love for God by our faith and trust in Him. A faith and trust which is proven by our obedience. Furthermore we must remember that, just like our earthy parents, our heavenly Father disciplines us when we disobey. In the book of Proverbs we are told: *"My son, do not reject the discipline of the LORD or loathe His reproof, for whom the LORD loves He reproves, even as a father corrects the son in whom he delights."* (Proverbs 3:11,12)

In Acts 5 we see the story of Ananias and Sapphira; a husband and wife who sold a piece of property and gave part of the money to the church. They told the Apostles that they were giving **all** the money from the sale of the property, but they lied. They kept a portion of that money for themselves. There was nothing wrong with keeping some of the money, the problem was they lied. The Apostle Peter announced *"You have not lied to men but to God."* (Acts 5:4) Their punishment was swift; they dropped dead on the spot. Obviously our heavenly Father doesn't punish everyone so severely, but this was a lesson to the church about how serious God views sin.

When asked what was the greatest commandment, Jesus answered *"You shall love the Lord your God with all your heart, and with all your soul, and with all your mind."* (Matthew 22:37) We love God by obeying Him with all our heart, soul and mind. Even our thoughts are to be obedient to God, but we have a stumbling block. We may be born again spiritually, but we still inhabit our sinful flesh. While we exist in these bodies, sin still remains in our thoughts and desires. Yet there is hope, because if we live *"in the Spirit"* we will gain control over our sinful flesh.

This is where Christians stand apart from unbelievers. God's Holy Spirit lives within us and we are commanded to live *"in the Spirit."* The Apostle Paul shows the vast difference between those of us who have been born again and those who remain dead in their sins: *"For those who* are according to the flesh set their minds on the things of the flesh, but those who are according to the Spirit, the things of the Spirit. For the mind set on the flesh is death, but the mind set on the Spirit is life and peace, because the mind set on the flesh is hostile toward God; for it does not subject itself to the law of God, for it is not even able to do so, and those who are in the flesh **cannot please God**." (Romans 8:5-8)

Those who are born again are *"new creatures"* and we set our minds on *"the things of the Spirit."* We do this when we obey God and not the sin that remains in our flesh. Unbelievers *"cannot please God"* because all they can do is live in the flesh and disobey God. We are now *"children of God"* and our thoughts and actions should reflect this. The Apostle Peter reminds us of this: *"As obedient children, do not be conformed to the former lusts which were yours in your ignorance, but like the Holy One who called you, be holy yourselves also in all your behavior; because it is written, YOU SHALL BE HOLY, FOR I AM HOLY."* (1 Peter 1:14-16)

So how do we live *"in the Spirit?"* We do this by immersing ourselves in the word of God. By reading and studying the Bible. The Holy Spirit within us is the Teacher who helps us to understand the meaning of Scripture. The more we read and study the Bible, the more the word of God permeates our thoughts. I believe that the Holy Spirit helps bring Scripture to mind so we can make our decisions Biblically. Therefore we can choose to obey God instead of our sinful flesh. The Apostle Paul warns us: *"Do not grieve the Holy Spirit of God."* (Ephesians 4:30) and *"Do not quench the Spirit."* (1 Thessalonians 5:19) We do this when we live *"in the flesh"* and not *"in the Spirit."* The Holy Spirit within us calls us to life, while the sin within us calls us to death. Hence the battle within. If we are truly born again our sins are forgiven; past, present and future. Yet the born again live to please God and when we win the battle over sin, this is pleasing to our heavenly Father and gives Him glory.

A study of Scripture shows that dealing with sin is one of the most important things a Christian has to do in life. Scripture is full of warnings about the dangers of sin and not dealing with it. The Apostle Paul encourages us to *"work out your own salvation with fear and trembling."* (*Philippians 2:12*) I believe that he was talking about being obedient to the commands of our Lord, with repentance being a major part of that obedience.

You may have heard the cliche 'Let go and let God,' but God isn't going to live your Christian life for you. We have to choose whether we obey God or whether we obey sin. A perfect example of this was the Apostle Paul when he said *"I discipline my body and make it my slave."* (*1 Corinthians 9:27*) Here was a man who was living *"in the Spirit."* He chose to resist the seductions of sin in his flesh and be obedient to God. He understood that he was the one who had to control his desires, God wasn't going to do it for him. We are the ones in charge of our decisions and we choose either to sin or to be obedient to God. Paul wasn't perfect and there were times when he too fell into sin, as we all will. Yet sin was no longer his way of life. We all fall at times, but when we do, we repent and confess our sins and God is faithful to forgive us. The Apostle John teaches: *"If we confess our sins, He is faithful and righteous to forgive us our sins and cleanse us from all unrighteousness."* (*1 John 1:9*)

Living the Christian life is not mystical, it's practical. When our minds are saturated with the word of God, all our decisions can be made in accordance with God's will. If we think Biblically we can know what is pleasing to our heavenly Father. To focus on God and His kingdom should always be our priority.

There was a point in the life of Jesus when He asked the disciples *"Who do you say that I am?"* (Matthew 16:15, Mark 8:29 & Luke 9:20) Peter answered correctly. He said *"You are the Christ."* Jesus responded to Peter by saying *"Blessed are you, Simon Barjona, because flesh and blood did not reveal this to you, but My Father who is in heaven."* (Matthew 16:17) After this incident Jesus was teaching the disciples about His impending death. Peter took Jesus aside and actually began to rebuke the Son of God. Jesus then scolded Peter with these words: *"Get behind Me, Satan; for you are not setting your mind on God's interests, but on man's."* (Mark 8:30 & Matthew 16:23) I'm sure that was a shock to Peter. One minute the Lord was blessing him and the next He was scolding him. The word *"Satan"* means adversary and it is the name given to the devil. Jesus called Peter *"Satan"* because he was acting like the devil. Peter was looking at things from his own point of view and not God's.

When we are living *"in the Spirit"* we set our minds on God's interests and not our own. Every decision we make will be made with the thought of obeying, pleasing and glorifying our heavenly Father. This takes time and effort, but the incredible benefit of living this way is that it will be a good indication that you are truly born again. So ask yourself, 'Am I living *"in the Spirit,"* or am I living *"in the flesh?"* Are you fighting this battle against sin? If you are,

I encourage you to keep fighting, because victory always comes through Jesus Christ in the power of the Holy Spirit. If you are not fighting sin, but obeying your sinful desires, then I urge you to get in the battle. Again I say, there is always victory through Jesus Christ.

Enemy Territory

If the world hates you, you know that it has hated Me before it hated you (John 15:18)

In the previous chapter we spoke about the sin that remains in our flesh, but this isn't the only enemy we fight. This world is drowning in sin. The devil, his demons, the world around us and even our own human nature all entice us to sin. We must remember that the devil is *"the ruler of this world." (John 12:31, 14:30 & 16:11)* Do you understand what this means? It means that we are currently living in the midst of Satan's kingdom, or as the Bible calls it, *"the domain of darkness." (Colossians 1:13)* We are actually living in enemy territory. Whether it's politics, science, entertainment, or even religion, everything is under the influence of the devil. The Apostle John tells us the devil *"deceives the whole world." (Revelation 12:9)* Sadly, the world we live in has fallen prey to the lies of the devil and readily believes his lies. This is why they don't see sin for what it really is. This is why they gladly believe such fabrications as mankind evolving from monkeys. Satan doesn't want the world to know that God is our Creator.

He doesn't want people to know that God created man in His image and he definitely doesn't want us to know that God is our Judge.

Let me remind you that we are at war. Spiritual war. A war between God and the devil. Each time we sin, this is a battle lost. However, each time we resist the temptation to sin, this is a battle won and Satan is defeated. Each time we win the battle against sin God is glorified. Winning more and more battles is a great indication of who's side we are on. It shows that we are maturing as Christians. Let us not forget that *"greater is He who is in you than he who is in the world."* (1 John 4:4) In other words, the Holy Spirit that dwells within us is far greater and more powerful than the devil who rules this world. In fact the Holy Spirit is more powerful than all the evil in this world. When we are led by the Holy Spirit we pursue righteousness, but when we are led by the devil we pursue unrighteousness. The more we pursue righteousness, the more confidence we have that we are truly born again.

As believers, we fight against the lies of the devil, because we fight for the truth. Biblical truth, the truth of God, is constantly being assaulted, but how many people who call themselves Christian stand up for the truth? Satan is so seductive in his deceptions that he has even influenced professing Christians into believing his lies. Unfortunately it seems that some who call themselves Christian would prefer to offend Holy God rather than the unsaved world. They don't want to stand up for Biblical truth because they feel intimidated by the world, or even worse, they believe the lies.

Scripture commands us through the Apostle Paul: *"Do not be conformed to this world, but be transformed by the renewing of your mind, so that you may prove what the will of God is, that which is good and acceptable and perfect."* (Romans 12:2) In the previous chapter we spoke of living *"in the Spirit"* by saturating our minds with holy Scripture. This is what Paul means when he says *"be transformed by the renewing of your mind."* When the word of God dominates our thoughts it is much easier to know the will of God and detect the lies of the devil.

Why are we commanded to *"not be conformed to this world?"* Because we have been taken out of this *"domain of darkness"* and placed into the kingdom of God. This world is marked for destruction. It is a dying world. In fact it is a world of death. Christians do not belong to this world, because we have been given the gift of eternal life. Therefore this world will hate us, just as it hated the Lord Jesus Christ. Jesus warned us of this: *"If you were of the world, the world would love its own; but because you are not of the world, but I chose you out of the world, because of this the world hates you."* (John 15:19)

We may be hated by the world, but we are loved by God. The suffering we experience in this life is a small price to pay compared to what God has prepared for us when we leave this world. Remember that we are on this planet for a very short time compared to eternity in paradise. The Apostle Paul encourages us when he says: *"For I consider that the sufferings of this present time are not worthy to be compared with the glory that is to be revealed to us."* (Romans 8:18) We must remember that we are just passing through this world on our way to our eternal home and we are commanded in Scripture to separate ourselves from this world and it's evil system. The Apostle John says *"Do not love the world nor the things in the world. If anyone loves the world, the love of the Father is not in him."* (1 John 2:15)

We have to ask ourselves 'Are our affections in this world or in heaven? Do we look forward to heaven, or are we so comfortable in this world that heaven holds no interest for us?' The Apostle Paul encourages us to *"Set your mind on the things above, not on the things that are on earth. For you have died and your life is hidden with Christ in God."* (Colossians 3:2,3) If we are born again our old life of living for ourselves has ended. Our old self has died with Christ on the cross and our new life is in Christ. Therefore, just like Jesus, we live to do the will of the Father. We live for the kingdom of God and not for the pleasures of this world.

Jesus informs us; *"For I have come down from heaven, not to do My own will, but the will of Him who sent Me."* (John 6:38) Therefore if we are true Christians, if we really are born again, we will follow in the footsteps of our Lord and always strive to do the will of our heavenly Father. Jesus tells us that we are in the family of God if we do so: *"For whoever does the will of My Father who is in heaven, he is My brother and sister and mother."* (Matthew 12:50, Mark 3:34, Luke 8:21)

We have to remember that we have died to our old sinful self and to this world. Jesus said *"If anyone wishes to come after Me, he must deny himself, and take up his cross daily and follow Me."* (Matthew 16:24, Mark 8:34 & Luke 9:23) Did you notice the word *"daily"* there? This means that we fight this battle every single day and we are always on guard for the deceptions of the devil. We are to follow our Lord and Savior and live as He lived in this world; in obedience to the Father. We are to deny the desires of our sinful flesh and live for the glory of God.

As we noted in the previous chapter, living the Christian life is practical. The more we study Scripture and obey the commands of our Lord, the more the word of God dominates our thoughts and matures us as Christians. The Apostle Paul tells us; *"we are no longer to be children, tossed here and there by waves and carried about by every wind of doctrine, by the trickery of men, by craftiness in deceitful scheming."* *(Ephesians 4:14)* If we live and breathe Scripture we will not be fooled by the devil and his servants.

I believe there are four simple rules to follow when living the Christian life:

1. If the Bible says do it, then do it.
2. If the Bible says don't do it, then don't do it.
3. Always compare what you are being told with what the Bible teaches.
4. If it's not in the Bible, don't trust it.

The first two rules are self explanatory, but what about the third rule? If we know our Bible well, we can refute many of the strange stories that claim to be Christian. A friend once told me about a man who apparently died and went to hell and then went to heaven and then came back to life. The story sounded very spiritual, but was it? In the gospel of Luke Jesus is telling the story of a beggar named Lazarus and a rich man. Lazarus goes to heaven and the rich man goes to hell. The rich man has a conversation with Abraham, who is in heaven. Abraham tells the man *"between us and you there is a great chasm fixed, so that those who wish to come over from here to you will not be able, and that none may cross over from there to us."* (Luke 16:26) This shows that no-one goes from hell to heaven or visa versa. Scripture is always the source of truth. Even the most spiritual sounding stories can be lies.

What do I mean by that fourth rule? It seems that many professing Christians are ready to believe almost anything these days. We see some within the Charismatic movement laughing uncontrollably, going into convulsions, or falling to the ground in what they call being 'slain in the spirit.' Are any of these things Biblical? No, not at all. These people will say "Just because it's not in the Bible, doesn't mean it's not true." I totally agree with that statement, but the safest place for a Christian is to compare everything we see and hear to holy Scripture. Scripture is always our source of truth. Claiming something to be Christian when it is not in the Bible is a dangerous place to be. Claiming something to be from the Holy Spirit, when in fact it is not, is a very dangerous place to be. Christians should always live in the confines of holy Scripture. This is the only safe place where we can confirm what is pleasing to our Lord.

The Pharisees were the enemies of Jesus. When speaking of Jesus they claimed that *"This man casts out demons only by Beelzebul the ruler of the demons."* (Matthew 12:24) They claimed that the power of Jesus came from the devil. Our Lord responded with *"any sin and blasphemy shall be forgiven people, but blasphemy against the Spirit shall not be forgiven."* (Matthew 12:31) The Pharisees were blaspheming the Holy Spirit, because they were claiming that it was the power of the devil and not the power of the Holy Spirit that Jesus used to cast out demons. What if people these days are claiming that certain things are the power of the Holy Spirit, when in fact it is the power of Satan? This too is blaspheming the Holy Spirit and as Jesus warned, this *"shall not be forgiven."*

The further churches stray from the Bible, the further they stray from the truth. If we are not living according to the word of God, how can we live in obedience to the Lord Jesus Christ? The Apostle John informs us that Jesus **is** *"the Word of God"* who *"became flesh."* (John 1:1 & 1:14) Jesus said *"He who eats My flesh and drinks My blood has eternal life."* (John 6:54) When we take in the word of God, we are taking in the word that reveals Christ. Our Lord confirmed this: *"You search the Scriptures because you think that in them you have eternal life, it is those that testify about Me."* (John 5:39) The Apostle Peter encourages us when he says *"like newborn babies, long for the pure milk of the word, so that by it you may grow in respect to salvation."* (1 Peter 2:2) We all know that newborn babies crave nothing more than their mother's milk. We are to long for the word of God with that same craving.

If we are to live in the truth and reject the lies of the devil and the world around us, we need to know Scripture intimately. I cannot stress this enough. If you have been born again you are now spiritually alive to God and your spiritual food **is** the word of God. Without it you will starve spiritually and allow the devil to make ground in your life. The great prophet Moses tells us that *"man does not live by bread alone, but man lives by everything that proceeds out of the mouth of the LORD."* (Deuteronomy 8:3) The Bible is the word of God *"that proceeds out of the mouth of the LORD."*

Study of Scripture gives us the desire to separate ourselves from the world. We are in the world, but we are not to be the same as the unsaved people of this world. How significant is this world to you? What if Christ returned tomorrow? Would you be jumping for joy, or would it bother you because you had plans for your life? So ask yourself 'Am I setting my affections on this world, or on heaven? Am I living in the flesh or in the Spirit? Am I denying my sinful flesh and living for Christ?' If we are living lives that are no different from the unsaved people around us, are we really born again? We have to ask ourselves 'Do we love this world and the things in it?' or 'Do we truly love God and reject this world?'

We should all be familiar with the parable of the soils. Sadly, it seems that many people who call themselves Christian fall into the category of the seed than fell among the thorns. Hear the words of our Lord Jesus: *"And others are the ones on whom seed was sown among the thorns; these are the ones who have heard the word, but the worries of the world, and the deceitfulness of riches, and the desires for other things enter in and choke the word, and it becomes unfruitful."* (Mark 4:18,19, Matthew 13:22)

Are you unfruitful as a Christian because you are worried about your life in this world? Are you more concerned with gaining wealth and material possessions than serving the Lord? Do you spend your time on worldly pursuits rather than reading and studying your Bible and being obedient to God? Do you believe the world or do you believe Scripture? We have to ask ourselves these questions and answer them honestly, because the answer to these questions will indicate whether we are truly born again.

Not of this World

You are a chosen race, a royal priesthood, a holy nation, a people for God's own possession. (1 Peter 2:9)

How strange are we compared to the unsaved world around us? They live for all they can get out of this world, whereas we live for the glory that is to come when we leave this world. The day will come when this entire universe will be destroyed and God will create a new heaven and a new earth. The holy city, the new Jerusalem, will come down from heaven and be placed onto the new earth. The writer of Hebrews tells us that Abraham *"was looking for the city which has foundations, whose architect and builder is God."* (Hebrews 11:10) This is the new Jerusalem spoken of in the book of Revelation. This is our eternal home.

However, it seems that so many professing Christians are so attached to this world that they don't care at all about our eternal home. They look for comfort and satisfaction in this world and seem to seek the same things the unsaved do. They involve themselves in worldly pursuits so that study of the word of God and proclaiming the gospel is often forgotten. How many of the unsaved people around you know that you're a Christian? Are you slandered for not acting the same as them? Do they give you a hard time because you don't get drunk, do drugs, or watch pornography as they do? Or are you doing those same things?

Study of the early church in the New Testament shows that Christians were persecuted for their faith. In fact Christians throughout history were persecuted for their faith. They were often shunned from the societies they lived in. Becoming a Christian meant that you could lose your family, your business and even your life. Being a Christian often resulted in suffering for the cause of Christ. The Apostle Peter encourages us with these words: *"If you are reviled for the name of Christ, you are blessed, because the Spirit of glory and of God rests on you."* (1 Peter 4:14)

The Apostle Peter understood what it was like to be *"reviled for the name of Christ"* and yet he rejoiced in his suffering. Peter and John were arrested and taken before the High Priest and the Council. The Council *"flogged them and ordered them not to speak in the name of Jesus, and then released them. So they* (Peter and John) *went on their way from the presence of the Council,* **rejoicing that they had been considered worthy to suffer shame for His name.**" (Acts 5:40,41) Is this your attitude, or do you shy away from conversations about Jesus with unbelievers for fear of their opinion of you? Do you rejoice when unbelievers harass, intimidate or abuse you?

Jesus warned His disciples many times that they would suffer for His name. He even told them *"an hour is coming for everyone who kills you to think that he is offering service to God."* (John 16:2) You see, as Christians, we are not of this world. Jesus tells us *"If you were of the world, the world would love its own; but because you are not of the world, but I chose you out of the world, because of this the world hates you."* (John 15:18,19) We should never fear the hatred of the world, because we have a future that far surpasses any suffering we endure in this world. As we noted in the previous chapter, the Apostle Paul gives wisdom when he says *"For I consider that the sufferings of this present time are not worthy to be compared with the glory that is to be revealed to us."* (Romans 8:18)

Whatever this world throws at us, we are to live in peace, love and humility. The Bible has much to say about pride and humility. Jesus tells the story of a proud man and a humble man: *"Two men went up into the temple to pray, one a Pharisee and the other a tax collector. The Pharisee stood and was praying this to himself: 'God, I thank You that I am not like other people; swindlers, unjust, adulterers, or even like this tax collector. I fast twice a week; I pay tithes of all that I get. But the tax collector, standing some distance away, was even unwilling to lift up his eyes to heaven, but was beating his breast, saying, 'God, be merciful to me, the sinner!' I tell you, this man went to his house justified rather than the other; for everyone who exalts himself will be humbled, but he who humbles himself will be exalted."* (Luke 18:10-14)

The Pharisee had confidence in his own self-righteousness and didn't consider his sinfulness. Yet the tax collector was fully aware of his sinfulness and called upon the mercy of God. This is the only attitude we can have to be saved.

Our own human righteousness cannot save us, only the righteousness of God through Jesus Christ can save us.

A friend once told me "When God looks at me He sees Jesus Christ." To be honest, I found this shocking. God does not look upon a Christian and see His sinless Son. He sees a sinner who is **covered by the righteousness** of His sinless Son. Think of it this way; imagine you're wrapped in a blanket and written all over this blanket is 'My sin.' Jesus is also wrapped in a blanket and written all over His blanket is 'The righteousness of God.' When you put your faith in Jesus Christ you trade blankets, so to speak. You're still a sinner, but now you're covered by the righteousness of God. Jesus is still the sinless Son of God and yet He took your sins upon Himself and paid the penalty for those sins. We must never think that we are something we are not. The Apostle Paul tells us *"I say to everyone among you not to think more highly of himself than he ought to think."* (Romans 12:3)

Have you ever noticed how people love to put others down to make themselves feel superior? It always disgusts me to see Christians doing this. I remember my mother being upset with women who gather in the carpark after church to gossip about others in the church. Where is the love? Where is the humility? So often we see Christians putting down unbelievers for not acting like Christians. We must remember that unbelievers **can't** act like Christians, because they are spiritually dead. They do not have the Holy Spirit living within them. They do not have the law of God written on their hearts. We must have a love for the lost and point them to the salvation that can be theirs by faith in Jesus Christ. We are not here to judge them, but to point them to the Lord Jesus Christ.

So many Christians judge unbelievers and yet we are commanded not to do so. In fact, we are commanded only to judge those inside the church, because it is those in the church who know the truth and should be living in accordance with God's commandments. When the Apostle Paul rebuked the Corinthian church for allowing sinful behavior within the congregation, he said *"I wrote you in my letter not to associate with immoral people; I did not at all mean with the immoral people of this world, or with the covetous and swindlers, or with idolaters, for then you would have to go out of the world. But actually, I wrote to you not to associate with any so-called brother if he is an immoral person, or covetous, or an idolater, or a reviler, or a drunkard, or a swindler - not even to eat with such a one. For what have I do do with judging outsiders? Do you not judge those who are within the church? But those who are outside, God judges. Remove the wicked man from among yourselves."* (1 Corinthians 5:9-13) Judgement of non-believers belongs to God, not us. We are to judge those who proclaim to be Christians in order to give them a chance to repent from their sin. If we point out a fellow believer's sin and they are repentant, then we gladly receive them back into the family.

Sadly, too many churches these days are not dealing with sin within the congregation. Our Lord Jesus gave instructions for how we deal with sin in the church. He said *"If your brother sins, go and show him his fault in private; if he listens to you, you have won your brother. But if he does not listen to you, take one or two more with you, so that by the mouth of two or three witnesses every fact may be confirmed. If he refuses to listen to them, tell it to the church; and if he refuses to listen even to the church, let him be to you as a Gentile and a tax collector."* (Matthew 18:15-17) In other words, remove him from the congregation. The church is the body of Christ and a stain on the body of Christ is a stain on Christ Himself. The church is to be pure, as Christ is pure.

The purity of the church is of utmost importance. We are to be so distinct from the world around us that they cannot ignore how completely different we are to them. What kind of testimony do we have when we appear to be exactly the same as the unsaved? We are to behave in a way that looks unnatural to the unbelieving world. We are to show them the beauty of salvation. We are to show that sin leads to destruction, but faith in Jesus Christ leads to eternal life. We are to show that the ways of the world are completely opposite to the ways of God. We are never to be selfish or unloving. We are to be humble and always show kindness to others. The Apostle Paul says *"Do nothing from selfishness or empty conceit, but with humility of mind regard one another as more important than yourselves."* (Philippians 2:3) As always, Jesus is our role model. *"For even the Son of Man did not come to be served, but to serve, and to give His life a ransom for many."* (Mark 10:45)

On the night before His crucifixion Jesus and the disciples were eating the passover meal. Jesus got up and went around to all the disciples and washed their feet. This was a job that the lowest household slave would normally do, so why did Jesus do this? To give an example and teach a very powerful lesson. *"So when He had washed their feet, and taken His garments and reclined at the table again, He said to them, "Do you know what I have done to you? You call Me Teacher and Lord; and you are right, for so I am. If I then, the Lord and the Teacher, washed your feet, you also ought to wash one another's feet. For I gave you an example that you also should do as I did to you."* (John 13:12-14)

As Christians we are to have a servant attitude. Jesus tells us *"If anyone wants to be first, he shall be last of all and servant of all."* (Mark 9:35) Pride is such an ugly human trait. Pride is at the root of all sin. How can we show the love of Jesus Christ to the world if we consider ourselves better than them? We must remember that if it wasn't for the grace and mercy of God we would be damned and on our way to hell, just like the unsaved.

Therefore, we must ask ourselves 'Are we behaving like unbelievers, or are we behaving like Jesus Christ? Does the world hate you for your faith, or do they not even know that you're a Christian? Do you treat unbelievers with disdain, or with love? Is the love of God within you? Are you showing this love to the world?' We show the world that we possess the love of God, which is a supernatural love. It is by this love that we show the attractiveness of Christ. Only Christians can show the love of God to the world. This is a predominant way in which we can show that we are truly born again.

Who Do You Love?

The one who does not love does not know God, for God is love. (1 John 4:8)

What is the driving force behind everything we do as Christians? How do we show the unsaved world around us that we are not like them? Love. Love for the Father and Jesus Christ, love for our fellow Christians, love for the unsaved and even love for our enemies. The Apostle John says *"See how great a love the Father has bestowed on us, that we would be called children of God; as such we are."* (1 John 3:1) Therefore, if we are now *"children of God"* we should love as our heavenly Father does and not like unbelievers, who the Apostle John calls *"children of the devil."* (1 John 3:10)

So we must ask ourselves, 'Do we love like God loves?' We should remind ourselves that God loved us when we were His enemies. The Apostle Paul reveals *"God demonstrates His own love toward us, in that while we were yet sinners, Christ died for us."* (Romans 5:8) Paul explains that *"while we were enemies we were reconciled to God through the death of His Son."* (Romans 5:10)

We have previously spoken about how we show love to God and Jesus Christ. We do this by our obedience, but what about love for other people? We can put people into two categories: Christians and unbelievers. We show a special love towards other Christians, because they are members of our spiritual family, but we also show love to unbelievers as an example of the love of God to them.

Christians have a special love for each other, because we are brothers and sisters in Christ. We are family. In fact we are the body of Christ and we all serve as different functions within that body. On the night before He was crucified, our Lord Jesus told the disciples *"A new commandment I give to you, that you love one another, even as I have loved you, that you also love one another. By this all men will know that you are My disciples, if you have love for one another."* (John 13:34,35) Our testimony to the world is our love for each other as Christians.

How had the Lord loved the disciples? Obviously in many ways, but in this instance He had just washed their feet. This was a task usually performed by the lowest household servant. Jesus was showing the disciples that they were to serve each other in love and humility. Showing love by serving our fellow Christians shows the world that we belong to Christ.

In the book of Acts we see this beautifully portrayed; *"the congregation of those who believed were of one heart and soul; and not one of them claimed that anything belonging to him was his own, but all things were common property to them."* and further; *"**For there was not a needy person among them,** for all who were owners of land or houses would sell them and bring the proceeds of the sales and lay* them at the apostles' feet, and they would be distributed to each as any had need." (Acts 4:32 & 4:34,35)

Can you imagine what a beautiful testimony we would have to the world if Christians these days behaved in this way? We would stand out among the rest of the world in a way that would be impossible to ignore. Sadly the world's values have encroached into the modern church and the selflessness of the early church is disappearing. How many of us are even aware of the needs of our fellow Christians? The New Testament is full of exhortations for us to display love for each other as Christians. To exhibit the incredible brotherly love that the early church displayed would shine a light to the world that would see them come running to discover what this love is. Why are we commanded to love in this way? The Apostle John gives us the simple answer: *"Beloved, if God so loved us, we also ought to love one another."* (1 John 4:11) If we are now *"children of God,"* we should love as God loves. Do you love your fellow Christians like people of the early church did? Do you love as God loves? Do you share what you have with others, or do you cling to your possessions like unbelievers do?

James gives us practical advice when he says: *"If a brother or sister is without clothing and in need of daily food, and one of you says to them, "Go in peace, be warmed and be filled," and yet you do not give them what is necessary for their body, what use is that?"* (James 2:15,16) If it is in our power to help others in need, then we help them in tangible ways. We should do this for both Christians and unbelievers. This is our testimony to the world.

As Christians we are called not just to love other Christians, but we are called to love everyone. We have previously spoken of the greatest commandment, which is to *"love the Lord your God with all your heart, and with all your soul and with all your mind, and with all your strength."* (Mark 12:29,30, Matthew 22:37) Jesus continued that conversation and said the second greatest commandment was *"You shall love your neighbor as yourself."* (Mark 12:31, Matthew 22:39)

To love and obey God and to treat others in a way that we want to be treated is to show ourselves to be true Christians, to be truly born again. Obviously this is not easy when living in a world that hates us. Yet we are commanded to do so.

I'd like to stop here and speak about the word love. In English we only have one word for love. This is the word we use for all of our affections; for anything from our spouses to our cars to our sports teams. However, in the original Greek of the New Testament there are four different words used for love.

1. Storge - this is the love of natural affections, like love within a family. The love of parents for children, or brothers and sisters.
2. Phileo - this is also known as 'brotherly love.' It can be used of the love that Christians have for each other, but it can also encompass the love we have for our fellow humans.
3. Eros - this speaks of sensual, or romantic love. This is the love of physical attraction and sexual desire. The love of intimacy between a husband and wife.
4. Agape - this is the love that seeks the best for others without expecting anything back. It is doing good

for others simply because we choose to. It is the love of the will. It is the love that God has for us. He loves us because He chooses to and not because of anything we have done to deserve His love. After all, we are all sinners unworthy of His love.

Agape is the word most commonly used when we are commanded to love. Agape speaks of doing good to others, no matter what they do to us. It is the love of the will. We choose to love, not expecting anything in return. We love in this way because this is the way God loves. The unsaved world doesn't love like this. They sometimes love when they are loved, but when they are offended, that love quickly turns to vengeance, or even hate.

On the other hand, we are commanded to treat everyone with kindness, even if we are mistreated by them. The Lord Jesus commands us to *"Love your enemies and pray for those who persecute you."* (Matthew 5:44, Luke 6:27,28) Obviously we don't have an emotional attachment to our enemies, or even most of the people we interact with, but we can still be kind to them. We can still do good for them. The Apostle Paul quotes *Proverbs 25:21* when he says *"if your enemy is hungry, feed him, and if he is thirsty, give him a drink."* (Romans 12:20)

Part of showing love to others is never taking vengeance on them, even when they hurt us. The Apostle Paul tells us *"Never take your own revenge, beloved, but leave room for the wrath of God, for it is written, "vengeance is Mine, I will repay," says the Lord"* (Romans 12:19) To claim revenge is what unbelievers do. The heroes of this world are the ones who repay their enemies with violence, but we are not like the world around us. Vengeance belongs to our heavenly Father and as the writer of Hebrews tells us: *"It is a terrifying thing to fall into the hands of the living God."* (Hebrews 10:31) When we take our own revenge we usually do this with a hateful, spiteful attitude, whereas when God takes vengeance He does so in perfect righteousness and justice.

In all things pertaining to the Christian life, Jesus is always our role model. When Jesus was nailed to the cross, He even prayed for forgiveness for those who put Him there. Can you imagine being nailed to a Roman cross and then looking into the faces of those who screamed for your blood and praying *"Father, forgive them; for they do not know what they are doing?"* (Luke 23:34) This kind of love takes a power that is beyond human. It is the power of God and if we really are born again, we are capable of showing this powerful love to the world.

When studying the New Testament you will find that Jesus never took vengeance on anyone, when He easily could have. You will also notice that He never got angry when He was dishonored. The only times you will find Him upset was when His Father, or the Holy Spirit was dishonored. The Apostle Paul behaved in exactly the same way. He was attacked from enemies without and enemies within and yet he never attacked back. He went through such pain and trials that we can't even comprehend, yet he always rested in the arms of his beloved God and Savior, Jesus Christ. He confronted sin and doctrinal error within the congregations, but he always did this with a fatherly love for the Christians under his authority.

The Apostle Peter encourages us when he says *"all of you be harmonious, sympathetic, brotherly, kindhearted, and humble in spirit; not returning evil for evil or insult for insult, but giving a blessing instead; for you were called for the very purpose that you might inherit a blessing."* (1 Peter 3:8,9) Our testimony to the world is that we love in a way that they can't comprehend. This type of love shows a strength that is supernatural. Natural human nature dictates that we hurt those who hurt us, but this is not how Christians are to behave. How many of us give a blessing when we are insulted? How many of us pray for those who are hateful towards us? It makes you realize just how far we are from how God wants us to be in this world.

One of the essential attributes of love is forgiveness. Forgiveness is central to the gospel. In fact it **is** the gospel. We show that we are truly born again when we forgive others as we have been forgiven by God. Jesus made this alarming statement: *"For if you forgive others for their transgressions, your heavenly Father will also forgive you. But if you **do not** forgive others, then your Father **will not** forgive your transgressions."* (Matthew 6:14,15) As Jesus clearly states here, if we don't forgive others, God won't forgive us. We show ourselves to be the true *"children of God"* when we forgive, because it is in God's nature to forgive.

Jesus tells us to; *"love your enemies, and do good, and lend, expecting nothing in return; and your reward will be great, and you will be sons of the Most High; for He Himself is kind to ungrateful and evil men. Be merciful, just as your Father is merciful."* (Luke 6:35,36) The Apostle Paul exhorts us to behave just like our Lord: *"So, as those who have been chosen of God, holy and beloved, put on a heart of compassion, kindness, humility, gentleness and patience; bearing with one another, and forgiving each other, whoever has a complaint against anyone; just as the Lord forgave you, so also should you."* (Colossians 3:12,13)

King David was God's chosen king of Israel. Scripture calls him *"a man after God's own heart,"* (1 Samuel 13:14, Acts 13:22) He shows this when he writes *"zeal for Your house has consumed me, and the reproaches of those who reproach You have fallen on me."* (Psalm 69:9) When Jesus cleansed the temple and drove out the money changers this Scripture was attributed to Him. So we must ask ourselves, 'Do we love others as God loves us? Do we take our revenge when others attack us, or do we leave vengeance to our heavenly Father? Are we offended when we are personally attacked, or are we offended when God is attacked?' The answers to these questions will tell us where our heart lies and this is a good indication of whether we are truly born again.

Sons of the Devil

You who are full of all deceit and fraud, you son of the devil, you enemy of all righteousness, will you not cease to make crooked the straight ways of the Lord? (Acts 13:10)

The Apostle Paul warned Timothy that *"the time will come when they will not endure sound doctrine; but wanting to have their ears tickled, they will accumulate for themselves teachers in accordance to their own desires, and will turn away their ears from the truth and will turn aside to myths."* (2 Timothy 4:3,4) That time is now. So many churches are sitting under teachers who don't present the truth of Scripture. Instead they manipulate the emotions of their listeners, or give motivational speeches that cater to the desires of the sinful flesh. They will throw in a Scripture verse or two to make their speeches sound Biblical, but they don't teach the truth of the word of God. Those who are truly born again find it hard to sit in churches like that and often leave to find a church that preaches the truth. We all need to be diligent in our study of the Bible, so we can be certain that we are being taught the truth.

If someone is preaching a gospel that is attractive to the sinful flesh, this is a false teacher preaching a false gospel. Some of these people present God as if He exists to serve us, when the opposite is true. I've even heard one false teacher claim that 'God isn't happy unless He's making you happy.' Such irreverence for Holy God is astounding and those lies will not go unpunished. Scripture is full of warnings against those who are the enemies of the gospel.

The Apostle Peter reminds us of this and the judgement that awaits false teachers: *"But false prophets also arose among the people, just as there will also be **false teachers among you**, who will secretly introduce destructive heresies, even denying the Master who bought them, bringing swift destruction upon themselves. **Many** will follow their sensuality, and because of them the way of the truth will be maligned; and in their greed they will exploit you with false words; **their judgement from long ago is not idle, and their destruction is not asleep.**"* (2 Peter 2:1-3) These false teachers will spend all eternity in torment, just like their father the devil. Peter tells us that *"many"* will follow these false teachers. Sadly they will follow these false teachers straight into the lake of fire, or as we call it, hell.

As we are speaking about eternal damnation, or hell, I would just like to clarify the truth of Satan's role there. So many people, Christians included, believe that Satan rules hell. This is not true. As Scripture clearly states, Satan is the ruler of **this** world. Hell is his eternal destination, but he won't be going there as ruler. He will be going there as the enemy of God who will be eternally tormented, as will everyone who is thrown into the lake of fire. In the first chapter of this book I told you about the final rebellion on earth against our Lord Jesus. A rebellion orchestrated by Satan. The Apostle John tells us *"they came up on the broad plain of the earth and surrounded the camp of the saints and the beloved city, and fire came down from heaven and devoured them. And the devil who deceived them was thrown into the lake of fire and brimstone, where the beast and the false prophet are also; and they will be tormented day and night forever and ever."* (Revelation 20:9,10) Scripture reveals that the devil, along with the beast and the false prophet, *"will be tormented day and night forever and ever."*

All who follow the devil will join him in this eternal torment. Jesus condemned the Pharisees as being sons of the devil when He proclaimed *"You are of your father the devil, and you want to do the desires of your father. He was a murderer from the beginning, and does not stand in the truth because there is no truth in him. Whenever he speaks a lie, he speaks from his own nature, for he is a liar and the father of lies."* (John 8:44)

Satan being *"the father of lies"* is also the great deceiver. The Apostle John calls him *"the serpent of old who is called the devil and Satan, who deceives the whole world."* (Revelation 12:9) False teachers are children of the devil who assist Satan with his deception. These people distort the truth of Scripture, or even oppose the truth of Scripture. They are on Christian radio, television, the internet and they are pastoring churches. Some of the most famous preachers and teachers in the world today are false teachers doing the work of their father the devil. A great sadness fills my heart when I see so many people following and believing these false teachers and their Satanic lies.

The devil knows that his time in this world is short and he is fully aware that he will spend all eternity in torment in the lake of fire. Satan has already been judged and he is not idle while awaiting his sentence. Knowing his eternal destiny, he is furious and wishes to take as many people with him as he can. The Apostle John informs us of this: *"Woe to the earth and the sea, because the devil has come down to you, having great wrath, knowing that he has only a short time."* (Revelation 12:12)

We must be aware that the devil not only does his work in the world around us, but he is extremely active in the church. Satan wants to keep as many people away from the truth as he can. He wants people to believe false gospels, so they are not truly saved. He wants to confuse weak Christians into believing false doctrines and lies. He wants to bring the world into the church, so that our testimony will be inadequate and unconvincing to the unbelieving world around us. Take a look at Christianity today. There are entire denominations who have turned their back on the word of God and now accept the lies of the devil. How is it possible for people who call themselves Christian to choose the lies of the devil over holy Scripture? We have to question if these people are born again.

The world has encroached so much into the church that the true church has largely disappeared. We know that God always keeps His remnant, the faithful who truly belong to Him, just like in ancient Israel when the prophet Elijah believed himself to be the only true worshipper of God. God told him *"I have kept for Myself seven thousand who have not bowed the knee to Baal."* (Romans 11:4, 1 Kings 19:18) Did you notice that God said *"I have kept for Myself?"* The Lord is always faithful to keep those who seek and obey Him. The faithful remnant will always strive to live in obedience to the Lord's commands. Rejecting sin and obeying God should be the life pattern of all those who are born again.

Ever since the church began it has been infiltrated by false teachers who have tried to cast doubts on the simple truth of the gospel. Jesus Himself was constantly battling with the religious leaders of His day and as we have previously noted, declared them to be sons of the devil. Jesus knew the hearts of these men and understood that they were seeking a righteousness of their own and not the righteousness of God that comes by faith. He even proclaimed a curse on them: *"But woe to you, scribes and Pharisees, hypocrites, because you shut off the kingdom of heaven from people; for you do not enter in yourselves, nor do you allow those who are entering to go in. Woe to you, scribes and Pharisees, hypocrites, because you travel around on sea and land to make one proselyte; and when he becomes one, you make him twice as much a son of hell as yourselves."* (Matthew 23: 13 and 15) There are many who may appear to be pious and devout, but the truth is sometimes the opposite. Sadly these people teach others to follow them down the path of darkness that leads to eternal damnation.

The Apostle John gives us a timely warning: *"Beloved, do not believe every spirit, but test the spirits to see whether they are from God, because **many false prophets** have gone out into the world."* (1 John 4:1) We must be aware of the subtleties of false teachers. Once again I urge Christians to compare the word of God to what we are being taught in our churches and in the media. It seems that some false teachers are not even subtle in their deceptions. They preach sermons that cater to sinful, human pride. Pride can be so destructive in the life of the Christian. There are false teachers who claim that we are 'little gods' or even worse, that we are God Himself. This is outright blasphemy. We must remember that only through faith in the Lord Jesus Christ can we be adopted into the family of God. I am not God the Almighty and neither are you. In fact I would be terrified to even think of myself as God.

A common false gospel being promoted today is the so called 'prosperity gospel' which states that God wants to bless us with material wealth and prosperity. This is a false gospel that caters to the desires of sinful, worldly people. There are many warnings in Scripture for those who pursue material wealth. The Apostle John reminds us that *"The world is passing away, and also it's lusts; but the one who does the will of God lives forever."* (1 John 2:17) Obedience to God is far more valuable than any amount of material wealth. Besides, we cannot buy our way into heaven.

If we seek the earthly, if we seek wealth and material possessions, we have to ask ourselves if we are truly saved. Proof of our salvation is exposed by what we desire and what we invest in. Our Lord states *"for where your treasure is, there your heart will be also."* (Matthew 6:21, Luke 12:34) This is a great opportunity for self examination. Are we storing up treasures here on earth, or are we investing in the kingdom of God?

We must remember that we are not of this world. We must remember that we are not to live *"in the flesh,"* but live *"in the Spirit."* The Apostle Paul reminds us of who we are if we do so: *"So then, brethren, we are under obligation, not to the flesh, to live according to the flesh - for if you are living according to the flesh, you must die; but if by the Spirit you are putting to death the deeds of the body, you will live. For all who are being led by the Spirit of God, these are sons of God."* (Romans 8:12-14)

If we are *"being led by the Spirit of God"* we will strive to live in obedience to holy Scripture, because obedience to Scripture is obedience to the Word of God Himself, Jesus Christ. Jesus, being the Word, is the truth. He said *"I am the way, and the truth, and the life; no one comes to the Father but through Me."* (John 14:6) The Apostle John wrote *"I have no greater joy than this, to hear of my children walking in the truth."* (3 John 1:4) Walking in the truth can show the difference between true believers and false, between true teachers and false. The Bible has much to say about those who do not walk in the truth:

a. *"For the wrath of God is revealed from heaven against all ungodliness and unrighteousness of men who suppress the truth."* (Romans 1:18)
b. *"but to those who are selfishly ambitious and do not obey the truth, but obey unrighteousness, wrath and indignation."* (Romans 2:8)
c. *"For this reason God will send upon them a deluding influence so that they will believe what is false, in order that they all may be judged who did not believe the truth, but took pleasure in wickedness."* (2 Thessalonians 2:11,12)

Condemnation is what awaits those who do not obey the truth. Once again we show that obedience is the mark of a true Christian. When we see professing Christians living in disobedience to God, we have to question their salvation. The same goes with teachers who are teaching error and not the truth. The most insidious false teachers are the ones who mix truth with error. A false teacher who only teaches lies is very easy to expose, but just like their father the devil, false teachers will confuse their listeners with a mixture of truth and lies. Let us not forget that Satan actually quoted Scripture when tempting Jesus in the wilderness. The devil knows the Bible very well and will try to distort the truth of Scripture, as do those who serve him. This is why study of the word of God is so important. When we accurately handle the word of God we can see through the deceptions of false teachers.

In a previous chapter we noted how churches are not dealing with sin within the congregation. I honestly fear for people who sit in churches like this. If the church is not dealing with sin, how many people sitting in these churches are not dealing with sin in their own lives? False teachers who don't confront sin give their listeners a false sense of security of their salvation. To believe that you are born again when you are not has such horrific eternal consequences.

The Lord Jesus proclaimed *"If anyone wishes to come after Me, he must deny himself, and take up his cross daily and follow Me."* (Luke 5:27, Mark 8:34 & Matthew 16:24) False teachers don't speak about denying ourselves. They are quick to speak about the love of God, but they avoid speaking about the wrath of God. They don't speak about repentance, sin, judgement or the purity of the church. Why is this? Because teaching the hard truths of Scripture doesn't attract a crowd. These false teachers want to have as many followers as possible and the best way to do that is to tell sinful people exactly what they want to hear. These are the teachers that the Apostle Paul warned Timothy about in his second letter to Timothy. Sadly the world is flooded with these false teachers doing the work of the devil.

False teachers like to stroke the egos of their listeners. They try to lift up humanity, while at the same time, bring God down to a level that is more comfortable. They almost humanize God if you will. They don't teach the depravity of mankind. They don't teach just how far from God we have strayed. In the first chapter of the book of Romans we read the Apostle Paul's description of the descent of mankind into depravity. If we read the first six chapters of the book of Genesis we see just how quickly that descent was. This is the fall of mankind. This is the history of the human race. The fact that God even offers humanity a chance at redemption should cause all of us to praise our heavenly Father for His glorious grace and mercy.

False teachers are experts at manipulating the emotions of their listeners. They do this through various means such as music and man centered preaching. We don't come to Christ through our emotions, we come through knowledge of the truth. The truth of who God is and who we are. The truth that God is our Creator and human beings are created in His image. The truth that we have all violated God's holy law. The truth that violating God's law is called sin and sin is punished. The truth that we cannot save ourselves from this punishment, only God can, through faith in His Son Jesus Christ. The knowledge of this truth should lead us to fall to our knees in repentance and ask for the mercy and forgiveness that God offers. This is the knowledge of the truth of salvation which can be ours, only by the grace of God.

My hope is that through study of the word of God all Christians will be able to detect the lies of false teachers and expose those lies to their Christian brothers and sisters. The children of God battle the lies of the devil with the truth; the truth of Scripture. False teachers are children of the devil and we defeat those false teachers with the truth. If we are truly born again we cannot help but fight this battle. It is in our new nature. So let us always compare what we are being taught to the word of God and we can be assured of victory in this battle. God is glorified when we do this. Are you boldly standing up for the truth? Are you fighting against the lies of the devil and his children? If so, praise God, this is a great indication that you are truly born again.

The Great Commission

Go therefore and make disciples of all the nations, baptizing them in the name of the Father and the Son and the Holy Spirit, teaching them to observe all that I commanded you; and lo, I am with you always, even to the end of the age (Matthew 28:19,20)

Why do Christians remain in this world after we are saved? Why is it that God doesn't immediately take us out of this sinful world and lift us up to heaven? The answer is that we have a responsibility here on earth. We are to serve our Lord by being witnesses. We are witnesses to the truth of salvation. We are witnesses to Jesus Christ. The Apostle Paul asks *"How will they believe in Him whom they have not heard? And how will they hear without a preacher?"* (Romans 10:14) We remain on earth to preach the gospel and tell our human brothers and sisters how they too can be saved from the wrath to come and inherit eternal life.

Imagine you're standing on a sidewalk and there are some children playing on the road. They're laughing and having a fun time as children do, but they don't see what you see; a big truck coming down the road, heading towards them at great speed.

So what is the loving thing to do? Let the kids continue playing because they're having a good time, or warn them of the impending danger? Obviously the loving thing to do is warn them of the horrific consequences that awaits them if they stay on the road.

This is why preaching the gospel to the world is the Christian's act of love. We are warning people of the danger ahead, because they can't see it. They may be having a good time in their sin, but they are completely unaware of the consequences of that sin. We warn them of the terror that faces them if they don't turn from their sin and turn to faith in Jesus Christ.

God offers the gift of salvation to humanity, because of His love for humanity. The Apostle John tells us: *"For God so loved the world, that He gave His only begotten Son, that whoever believes in Him shall not perish, but have eternal life."* (John 3:16) It is our responsibility as Christians to show that same love by presenting the gospel to the world. This is the great commission. This is our calling. Do we have love for our fellow human beings? Are we presenting the gospel to the world around us? Because our ultimate act of love to the unsaved world is to tell them the truth of the gospel.

The Apostle Peter describes God as *"not wishing for any to perish but for all to come to repentance."* (2 Peter 3:9) The Apostle Paul describes our heavenly Father as *"God our Savior, who desires all men to be saved and to come to the knowledge of the truth."* (1 Timothy 2:3,4) If God desires all men to be saved, shouldn't we as His beloved children desire the same? Shouldn't we teach others the *"knowledge of the truth?"*

So where do we find this *"knowledge of the truth?"* Obviously in the word of God. What we do with this knowledge will determine our eternal destination. We can repent from our sins and come to faith in Jesus Christ, or we can continue in sin and suffer the consequences eternally in the lake of fire.

Preaching the gospel is not easy, especially in the world we live in. Christianity is being presented more and more as an extremist point of view. One secular news reporter even scoffed at the idea that homosexuality could be considered a sin. Apparently Holy God no longer determines what sin is, the unsaved world does. Of course if Christians disagree with unbelievers, we are labelled as being unenlightened, unloving or intolerant. I have always found it extremely hypocritical that a Biblical world view is seen as intolerant and yet to oppose, dishonor, or even humiliate that Biblical world view is not intolerant at all. Such are the double standards we live under in this unbelieving world.

So why is the gospel met with so much opposition and hostility? It is because human beings love their sin and they don't want to be told that they will be judged for that sin. Our Lord tells us *"This is the judgement, that the Light has come into the world, and men loved the darkness rather than the Light, for their deeds were evil. For everyone who does evil hates the Light, and does not come to the Light for fear that his deeds will be exposed."* (John 3:19, 20) Those people who reject the gospel would rather embrace their sin than Jesus Christ. They love their sin so much that they hate the idea of repenting and living in obedience to Holy God. The gospel is nothing short of foolishness to them and they can't understand why we would choose such a narrow path.

Christians are often seen as being narrow minded because of our declaration that Jesus Christ is the only way to heaven. Many people in the unbelieving world think that we can all choose our own path to heaven, but this is incorrect. Our Lord teaches us: *"Enter through the narrow gate; for the gate is wide and the way is broad that leads to destruction, and there are many who enter through it."* (Matthew 7:13) The vast majority of people in this world, both religious and non-religious, are on that wide path that leads to destruction. Many people believe themselves to be on the path to heaven, when in fact they are not.

To present the gospel we must make the unbelieving world aware that sin is a violation of God's law and there is a penalty for breaking that law. An eternal penalty. Take a look at the world around you. All that people are concerned with is their life in this world. The only thing they live for is this life and what they can get out of it. They honestly don't look at the big picture of eternity, or at least they don't want to. Life on this planet for most people is less than 100 years. That may seem like a long time, but when you compare that to the vastness of eternity, it's not even a drop in the ocean. Yet most people only live for the here and now. They don't understand that this life is a test. A test of faith. Our eternal destiny is determined by what we put our faith in, or rather, who. Do we believe the truth of Jesus Christ, or do we believe the lies of the devil? Do we put our faith in God through Jesus Christ, or do we put our faith in the devil? Faith in God through Jesus Christ results in eternal life, whereas faith in the devil results in eternal torment. The Apostle Peter informs us that *"there is salvation in no one else; for there is no other name under heaven that has been given among men by which we must be saved." (Acts 4:12)*

To live for the pleasures of the flesh in this life, only to spend all eternity in torment in the lake of fire, just seems ridiculous to all of us who are born again. To suffer in this life for the sake of Christ, this is a very small price to pay for the magnificence of eternal life that God offers. The Apostle Paul makes perfect sense when he says *"For I consider that the sufferings of this present time are not worthy to be compared with the glory that is to be revealed to us." (Romans 8:18)* And further in that same passage he says *"with perseverance we wait eagerly for it." (Romans 8:25)*

We know that we will suffer in this world, because it is a fallen world. Sometimes we suffer because we do evil and sometimes we suffer because we do good. The Apostle Peter tells us that we are called to suffer for good and this finds favor with God: *"For what credit is there if, when you sin and are harshly treated, you endure it with patience? But if when you do what is right and suffer for it you patiently endure it, this finds favor with God. For you have been called for this purpose, since Christ also suffered for you, leaving you and example for you to follow in His steps." (1 Peter 2:20,21)* Jesus only ever did good in this world and yet He suffered for it. We are called to be like Christ.

If you live as a slave to sin in this world, if you reject Jesus Christ, you will be condemned to an eternity of torment in the lake of fire. This is God's warning to the unbelieving world. This is where we begin the gospel. The word gospel means good news, but the good news is not complete without presenting the truth of eternal damnation. If the world is not aware of the terrors of hell, there is little motivation to embrace the salvation that God provides through His Son Jesus Christ. To inform the unbelieving world of the salvation that God offers, we have to tell them why they need to be saved and what they need to be saved from.

One of the predominant lies of the devil these days is that hell is some kind of big party. In hell you can do whatever you like and there is nobody to tell you otherwise. Ignorantly, people don't consider that in hell there will be rapists, murderers, child molesters and the like. So does that mean all those people will have the freedom to do whatever they like? Obviously. Isn't it strange that nobody ever thinks of that? Of course the real truth is that hell is not a party at all and nobody in hell gets to do whatever they like. Hell is a prison. In fact some people believe that it will be a prison of your own conscience. An idea that I personally find interesting.

As human beings we teach ourselves to neglect our consciences for the purpose of obeying and enjoying our sin. The conscience is a warning device that informs us of the spiritual damage we are doing because of sin. Yet we consistently reject and ignore our consciences for the purpose of enjoying our sin. Some people believe that those who are sent to hell will be sent there with a fully informed conscience that can't be ignored and it will be each person's own conscience that will be their tormentor. We cannot escape our own conscience.

In truth the Bible doesn't inform us as to how those in hell will be tormented. It simply states that they will be. We must remember that the Bible tells us what we need to know and not always what we want to know. We can rest in the fact that God has a purpose for this. God desires that we always focus on what is important here and now. Perhaps all of our questions will be answered in the life to come, but for now we must keep our focus on glorifying our Lord by being obedient to all He commands.

Hell, or the lake of fire, is described as *"outer darkness"* where there will be *"weeping and gnashing of teeth."* (Matthew 8:12, 22:13, 25:30) The torment that those in hell experience will be relentless and unending. Can you imagine living forever in torment? Never ending suffering with no relief. This is why we preach the gospel. This is why salvation is so precious. To be saved from unending torment is God's amazing gift to mankind. This is why those of us who are born again can't help but thank and praise God for His incredible grace and mercy. We have a debt that is impossible to pay, other than spending all eternity in the lake of fire. For God to send His beloved Son to pay that debt on our behalf is astounding. This is our message to the world. This is what we preach; the beautiful gospel. To be given a chance at redemption when we don't deserve it.

So I hope and pray that all who are truly born again are preaching the gospel. Let us preach the whole gospel; the good news and the bad news. After all, without the bad news, the good news is only half the message. We see so many professing Christians preaching that 'Jesus loves you,' but we need to explain just how Jesus showed that love: By coming to earth and becoming human, living a sinless life and dying on the cross for the sins of the world. The cross is the centre of the gospel. Without the cross there is no gospel. Jesus died on the cross for our sins. He rose again to show that He is the sinless Son of God and death has no power over Him. When we put our faith in Jesus we rise from the dead also. We rise again to new life, spiritual life in Jesus Christ. Without that new life we are eternally damned. Without that new life we are spiritually dead. We need to be born again.

True Worship

Beware of the dogs, beware of the evil workers, beware of the false circumcision; for we are the true circumcision, who worship in the Spirit of God and glory in Christ Jesus and put no confidence in the flesh (Philippians 3:2,3)

What is worship? I know that sounds like a strange question, but it seems that many Christians today feel that worship is not much more than singing songs in church. In fact some churches call their music director the 'Worship Leader.' Singing songs of praise is definitely an element of worship, but true worship goes much deeper. Our Lord Jesus said *"But an hour is coming, and now is, when the true worshipers will worship the Father in spirit and truth; for such people the Father seeks to be His worshipers. God is spirit, and those who worship Him must worship in spirit and truth."* (John 3:23,24)

As Jesus said, we *"must worship in spirit and truth."* It seems that many churches have a spirit for God, but little truth. This is why pastors and teachers should be teaching the word of God, the Bible. The Bible is the source of truth and it is through knowledge of the word that we are motivated to worship Holy God. The Bible is God revealing Himself to mankind. He reveals Himself as Creator, Lawgiver, Provider, Almighty, Patient, Everlasting, Shepherd, Healer, Savior and so much more. I believe the human mind cannot fully comprehend all that God truly is, yet God has given us His word to reveal Himself and what we need to know in this life. In particular, our need to repent and come to faith in the Lord. Even though we have all violated His laws, God still holds out His hand to us in love.

The Bible is where we learn the truth of God and Jesus Christ and the fact that we are to worship no-one else. The Bible clearly states that we are to worship God alone and yet we also worship Jesus. Our human minds separate the Father and Son as two individuals, which they are, and yet they are one. This is so hard for us to understand. How can two individuals be one? The fact is that they are one in nature. God the Father and God the Son. God the Father is Spirit and God the Son is that Spirit in human flesh.

The Apostle John tells us *"In the beginning was the Word, and the Word was with God, and the Word was God."* (John 1:1) The original Greek construction of that sentence goes like this: In the beginning was the Word, and the Word was with God, and **God was the Word.** It seems to have a little more clarity when written that way. Further in John's gospel he writes *"And the Word became flesh, and dwelt among us, and we saw His glory, glory as of the only begotten from the Father."* (John 1:14) The Apostle Paul speaks of "Christ Jesus, who, although He existed **in the form of God,** *did not regard equality with God a thing to be grasped, but emptied Himself, taking the form of a bond-servant, and being made in the likeness of men."* (Philippians 2:5-7)

It is hard for us to understand God walking around in His own creation in human flesh. It was hard for the people in the time of Jesus, as it has been hard for people ever since. Yet this is the truth. If Jesus were merely a human prophet He would not have accepted worship. Yet 'Matthew 2:11, Matthew 14:33, Matthew 28:16-17, John 9:35-38, John 20:28, Philippians 2:9-11 and Hebrews 1:6' all speak of the worship of Jesus Christ. The book of Revelation reveals the worship of Jesus as the Lamb of God. So we as Christians should feel comfortable worshipping Jesus Christ as well as God the Almighty. In fact it is to the glory of the Father that we do so.

So how do we worship? Once again we come back to obedience. Being obedient to the Word of God is an essential service and therefore worship of God. True obedience is from the heart and so is true worship. The Pharisees, who Jesus called *"sons of the devil,"* paraded themselves publicly as worshippers of God and yet this was not the case. They would announce their arrival with trumpets and made a spectacle of themselves when they prayed or gave money in the temple. Sadly, they were worshipping themselves and not God. Our Lord Jesus said *"Beware of practicing your righteousness before men to be noticed by them; otherwise you have no reward with your Father who is in heaven."* (Matthew 6:1) Jesus tells us *"Whoever exalts himself shall be humbled; and whoever humbles himself shall be exalted."* (Matthew 23:12, Luke 14:11)

The Old Testament prophet Samuel writes *"God sees not as man sees, for man looks at the outward appearance, but the Lord looks at the heart."* (1 Samuel 16:7) There are many people in the world who parade themselves as being religious and often outward appearances would show them to be worshippers of God, but this is not always the case. God knows who is truly transformed. He knows His true children, because He is the One who transformed them. He is the One who caused them to be born again. There are some in the world who might fool other people, or even themselves, but nobody fools God.

To worship our Lord in spirit and truth, we are to worship with humility. True worshippers don't pat themselves on the back for being holy and devout. True worshippers know that they are undeserving sinners who have been given the precious gift of eternal life. It honestly disgusts me when I see professing Christians being condescending towards the unsaved, or even other Christians. True Christians never feel superior to unbelievers. In fact they never feel superior to anyone. Humility is what marks someone who is truly born again. Understand that we did nothing to earn our salvation. We were not wise or spiritual enough to gain our salvation, because before we were born again, we were spiritually dead and thus incapable of anything spiritual. We were slaves to sin and by the grace of God we have been bought by the precious blood of Jesus Christ. Bought from the slave market of sin and placed into the kingdom of God.

The Apostle Paul makes this perfectly clear; *"do you not know that your body is a temple of the Holy Spirit who is in you, whom you have from God, and that* **you are not** *your own? For you have been **bought with a price**; therefore glorify God in your body."* (1 Corinthians 6:19,20) The Apostle Peter informs us of the price that was paid for our redemption; *"you were not redeemed with perishable things like silver or gold from your futile way of life inherited from your forefathers, but with precious blood, as of a lamb unblemished and spotless, the blood of Christ."* (1 Peter 1:18,19) True Christians are owned by God. We are bought and paid for with *"the blood of Christ."* This sounds like we are slaves and that is exactly what we are; slaves of Christ. There are only two types of people in this world; slaves to sin, or slaves to Christ. Do you serve sin, or do you serve Christ?

The Apostle Paul tells us that we give ourselves as a service of worship: *"Therefore I urge you, brethren, by the mercies of God, to present your bodies a living and holy sacrifice, acceptable to God, which is your spiritual service of worship."* (Romans 12:1) We are to present our bodies *"a living and holy sacrifice,"* which means that we are to be holy. The Apostle Peter exhorts us: *"As obedient children, do not be conformed to the former lusts which were yours in ignorance, but like the Holy One who called you, be holy yourselves also in all your behavior, because it is written,"YOU SHALL BE HOLY, FOR I AM HOLY."* (1 Peter 1:14-16)

The Apostle Paul teaches us: *"Therefore do not let sin reign in your mortal body so that you obey its lusts, and do not go on presenting the members of your body to sin as instruments of unrighteousness; but present yourselves to God as those alive from the dead, and your members as instruments of righteousness to God."* (Romans 6:12,13) Avoiding sin and unrighteousness and living a life of righteousness is what we are encouraged to do. James tells us: *"Submit therefore to God. Resist the devil and he will flee from you. Draw near to God and He will draw near to you."* (James 4:7,8) Resisting temptation is our daily battle. Drawing near to God through prayer and study of Scripture is our daily pursuit.

True Christians no longer serve sin, we serve the Lord. We no longer live to please our sinful flesh, we now live to please our heavenly Father. The Apostle Paul tells us that *"the body is not for immorality, but for the Lord, and the Lord is for the body."* (1 Corinthians 6:13) To be born again is to be one with Christ. The Apostle Paul reminds us: *"Do you not know that your bodies are members of Christ?"* (1 Corinthians 6:15) As Christians, we have an obligation to serve the Lord and not our sinful desires. Being *"members of Christ,"* do we dare allow His *"members"* to indulge in sin? Of course not. We are to follow our Lord and Savior and walk as Christ walked, in purity.

Those who are truly born again do not live in immorality as unbelieving people do. The Apostle John tells us: *"By this we know that we have come to know Him, if we keep His commandments. The one who says, "I have come to know Him," and does not keep His commandments, is a liar, and the truth is not in him; but whoever keeps His word, in him the love of God has truly been perfected. By this we know that we are in Him; the one who says he abides in Him ought himself to walk in the same manner as He walked."* (1 John 2:3-6) Once again we see obedience as the mark of a true Christian.

When it comes to worship, prayer is foundational. Communion with our heavenly Father is crucial to those who are *"children of God."* Sadly, like so many other facets of Christianity, prayer has become selfish, superficial and earth bound. We pray for material possessions and earthly comfort when we should be praying about spiritual matters instead. Scripture exhibits the Apostle Paul as one of the finest examples of a true Christian. If we study the prayers of Paul we don't see him praying selfishly, we see him praying spiritually. He always prays with his focus firmly on God. He prays that Christians will grow in knowledge of the truth and act accordingly as *"children of God."* He prays that the gospel will be proclaimed boldly throughout all the world. He never focuses his prayers on himself, unless it pertains to the gospel. He always focuses his prayers on the kingdom of God and expanding that kingdom. Paul sets a great example for us to follow.

Prayer is where we personally commune with God and this is a beautiful time when we can praise God from the heart, not just for what He has done in our lives, but for all He has done for humanity and all that He is. We praise God because He is God. Is He not worthy of praise? When I think of all that God has done, including His incredible plan of redemption, I can't help but be overwhelmed. It shows that we as humans are so far from God that the distance is immeasurable. The prophet Isaiah confirms this: *"For My thoughts are not your thoughts, nor are your ways My ways,"* declares the Lord. *"For as the heavens are higher than the earth, so are My ways higher than your ways and My thoughts higher than your thoughts."* (Isaiah 55:8,9) God sent His only Son to die for the sins of those who rejected Him and violated His law. Would we do the same? How magnificent is our God! How amazing is His grace!

There are times in our lives when we are compelled to dedicate ourselves deeper in prayer than at other times. These are the times when fasting is combined with prayer. In fact there are times when we are so deeply in communion with our heavenly Father that we naturally neglect food in favor of prayer. These are often times when we are questioning God's purpose for what is happening in our lives and we seek the face of God to answer those questions. These are often times when our faith is being tested.

One of the greatest opportunities we have for worship is when our faith is tested. The prophet Samuel relates the story of King David in such a time. David sinned by making love to the woman Bathsheba, knowing that she was married. Bathsheba became pregnant and when David found out he tried to get her husband Uriah to sleep with her, so that Uriah would believe that the child was his. Uriah was one of David's soldiers and he refused to enjoy pleasure with his wife while his fellow soldiers were fighting on the battlefield. So David had Uriah killed and took Bathsheba for his own wife. God punished David by striking the child of their union with sickness. David fasted and prostrated himself before the Lord for days. He sought God's mercy, but on the seventh day the child died. When David found out, Samuel tells us *"David arose from the ground, washed, anointed himself, and changed his clothes; and he came into the house of the LORD and **worshipped**."* (2 Samuel 12:20) God is worthy of worship, even when He doesn't answer our prayers as we would like.

The Apostle Peter gives us encouragement when we experience these times: *"In this you greatly rejoice, even though now for a little while, if necessary, you have been distressed by various trials, so that the proof of your faith, being more precious than gold which is perishable, even though tested by fire, may be found to result in praise and glory and honor at the revelation of Jesus Christ."* (1 Peter 1:6,7)

God tests our faith for a purpose. James, just like Peter, gives us encouragement and reveals that purpose: *"Consider it all joy, my brethren, when you encounter various trials, knowing that the testing of your faith produces endurance. And let endurance have its perfect result, so that you may be perfect and complete, lacking in nothing."* (James 1:2-4) The Apostle Paul expands on this; *"we exult in hope of the glory of God. And not only this, but we also exult in our tribulations, knowing that tribulation brings about perseverance; and perseverance, proven character; and proven character, hope; and hope does not disappoint, because the love of God has been poured out within our hearts through the Holy Spirit who was given to us."* (Romans 5:2-5) The Apostle Paul reminds us that *"God causes all things to work together for good to those who love God, to those who are called according to His purpose."* (Romans 8:28)

When our faith is tested and we are proven to be true Christians, our natural desire is to worship our Lord. To know that you are truly saved, truly born again, is reason to worship God in praise and thankfulness. When our faith is tested and proven, we are given encouragement that we will enter the kingdom of heaven. This inspires us to continue in obedience to the word of God. Let me remind you of the words of our Lord: *"Not everyone who says to Me, 'Lord, Lord,' will enter the kingdom of heaven, but he who does the will of My Father who is in heaven will enter."* (Matthew 7:21)

When we read and study the word of God there are times when we can't help but burst into praise. Have you ever found that in your life? You'll be reading Scripture and you find yourself amazed and overwhelmed by God and you find your heart overflowing with praise and gratitude to our heavenly Father. We worship our Lord with a heart of gratitude. When you are truly born again, it's hard not to be thankful for all that our Lord has done, both in our lives and in the lives of all those who have come to know Him throughout history. To see the love and patience that God displays to the human race is both heartwarming and soul stirring. Mankind became enemies of God and yet He chose to redeem the human race instead of destroying it.

To worship God is to worship the God who is love and I believe that we return that love to God by our obedience, praise, gratitude and worship. Are you overwhelmed by the love of God? Do you want to do all you can to be pleasing to our heavenly Father? If so, this is a good indication that you truly are born again.

Are You?

You will be hated by all because of My name, but the one who endures to the end, he will be saved (Mark 13:13)

Scripture is full of warnings to people who claim to be Christian, yet show no evidence of their transformation. The Bible reveals who is truly saved and who is not. The word of God could not be clearer. So again I exhort all professing Christians to read and study the Bible and be certain that they are on the narrow path that leads to eternal life.

We must remember that we cannot save ourselves. When we are given the gift of salvation we are covered by the righteousness of God through faith in Jesus Christ. When this happens a transformation occurs and we are sealed with the Holy Spirit of God, who takes up residence within us. Our Lord Jesus told a parable about a king who gave a wedding feast for his son. Those who were called to the feast all gave excuses for not attending, so the king sent out his slaves to gather anyone they could find: *"Those slaves went out into the streets and gathered together all they found, both evil and good; and the wedding hall was filled with dinner guests. But when the king came in to look over the dinner guests, he saw a man there who was not dressed in wedding clothes, and he said to him, 'Friend, how did you come in here without wedding clothes?' And the man was speechless. Then the king said to the servants, 'Bind him hand and foot, and throw him into the outer darkness; in that place there will be weeping and gnashing of teeth.' For many are called, but few are chosen." (Matthew 22:10-14)*

This was a parable that compared the king to God giving a feast for all those who love His Son, Jesus Christ. The Bible presents the church as the bride of Christ. Many are invited to the feast, but only those who are dressed appropriately can attend. Therefore, I believe this part of the parable shows that only those who are covered by the righteousness of God can gain entrance into the kingdom of heaven. This is shown by the man who was not dressed in wedding clothes. He was not covered by the righteousness of God. He was not sealed with the Holy Spirit, as all true believers are. We can look and act like Christians on the outside, but unless the Holy Spirit is within us, we are only fooling ourselves.

The Apostle Paul tells us the characteristics of those who have been sealed with the Holy Spirit; *"the fruit of the Spirit is love, joy, peace, patience, kindness, goodness, faithfulness, gentleness, self-control."* (Galatians 5:22,23) If you can see these characteristics growing in your life, this is a good indication that the Holy Spirit is working in you.

In contrast, Paul also tells us; *"the deeds of the flesh are evident, which are; immorality, impurity, sensuality, idolatry, sorcery, enmities, strife, jealousy, outbursts of anger, disputes,* *dissensions, factions, envying, drunkenness, carousing, and things like these, of which I forewarn you, just as I have forewarned you, that those who practice such things **will not inherit the kingdom of God**."* (Galatians 5:19-21) If the practice of your life is listed here, then eternal torment in the lake of fire is what awaits you.

The Apostle Paul teaches us who will not be going to heaven; *"do you not know that the unrighteous will not inherit the kingdom of God? Do not be deceived; neither fornicators, nor idolaters, nor adulterers, nor effeminate, nor homosexuals, nor thieves, nor the covetous, nor drunkards, nor revilers, nor swindlers, will inherit the kingdom of God."* (1 Corinthians 6:9,10) There are people who practice such things and still believe themselves to be Christian. How? How is it possible to completely ignore the word of God and fool yourself into believing a lie? Perhaps these people don't even read their Bibles. Perhaps they are being deceived by a false teacher they follow. The Bible exposes the truth about ourselves and our eternal destination. It also reveals much about our Creator.

We are all familiar with the love of God, but the Bible also reveals that there are things God hates. In the book of Proverbs we read: *"There are six things which the LORD hates, yes seven which are an abomination to Him: Haughty (prideful) eyes, a lying tongue, and hands that shed innocent blood, a heart that devises wicked plans, feet that run rapidly to evil, a false witness who utters lies, and one who spreads strife among brothers."* (Proverbs 6:16-19) If we look at the world around us we find all of these are commonplace. Scripture reveals how we are to conduct ourselves as Christians and how we are not to conduct ourselves.

The battle we fight against the devil, the world and even our own flesh is a daily battle and eternal life only comes to those who continue this fight to the end.

Our Lord Jesus give us encouragement in these difficult times: *"Many false prophets will arise and will mislead many. Because lawlessness is increased, most people's love will grow cold. But the one who endures to the end, he will be saved."* (Matthew 24:11-13) When we stand firm in our faith, when we continue to live in a way that is pleasing to our heavenly Father, we show ourselves to be truly saved. Jesus again gives us encouragement: *"You will be hated by all because of My name, but the one who endures to the end, he will be saved."* (Mark 13:13)

We fight this battle to the end of our lives here in this world. We never give up. We never let our guard down. Each new day is a new battle to fight. The enemy will launch assaults on us and look for times when we are at our weakest to launch the most aggressive assaults. Yet we rest in the loving arms of our Lord. We continue in obedience, knowing that the great Day of the Lord is coming to end this war forever. The great day when our Lord is glorified in victory.

In the gospels we read the Sermon on the Mount, where Jesus taught 'the Beatitudes.' Our Lord teaches us that we are blessed if we possess certain characteristics, or attitudes. I believe that Jesus is teaching us the characteristics of those who are truly born again. After all, if we are born again then we are truly blessed. The Beatitudes are a great study for Christians. If we can see ourselves there, this gives us great encouragement that we are on the path that leads to eternal life.

The Beatitudes:

> *Blessed are the poor in spirit, for theirs is the kingdom of heaven.*

The Greek word here for poor is 'ptōchos' and it speaks of extreme poverty, such as a beggar on the street who doesn't know when his next meal will come. All those who come to God for salvation understand that they are spiritually destitute. Unless God gives life to us spiritually, we are damned. Those who believe themselves to be good enough, wise enough, or spiritual enough to gain eternal life will not inherit the kingdom of heaven. King David reminds us what is pleasing to God: *"For You do not delight in sacrifice, otherwise I would give it; You are not pleased with burnt offering. The sacrifices of God are a broken spirit; a broken and a contrite heart, O God, You will not despise."* (Psalm 51:16,17)

> *Blessed are those who mourn, for they shall be comforted.*

We mourn over our own sinfulness as well as the sinfulness of the world. We mourn because God is dishonored by sin. I believe we also mourn because we know the truth when so many people reject the truth and therefore reject Jesus Christ. We mourn because we know those people will suffer eternal torment in the lake of fire. We mourn because we sometimes fall into sin, knowing that this dishonors and displeases our heavenly Father. When we look at the world through the eyes of God there is reason to mourn. In the gospels we see times when Jesus wept. The prophet Isaiah even describes Christ as *"a man of sorrows and acquainted with grief."* (Isaiah 53:3)

> *Blessed are the gentle (humble, meek), for they shall inherit the earth.*

Knowing that our Lord Jesus was humble, we long to be like Him. When we behave in the same manner as our Lord and Savior, this gives us encouragement that we are *"children of God."* Humility makes us stand out in this world. Jesus said: *"Take my yoke upon you and learn from Me, for I am gentle and humble in heart, and you will find rest for your souls."* (Matthew 11:29) The Apostle Paul encourages us: *"If possible, so far as it depends on you, be at peace with all men."* (Romans 12:18)

> *Blessed are those who hunger and thirst for righteousness, for they shall be satisfied.*

We love righteousness because our Lord is righteous and we long to be like Him. We understand that unrighteousness is the path that leads to eternal damnation. We look at the unrighteousness of this world and we long to see a world of righteousness. We long to leave the darkness of this world and live in the light of the glory of God the Almighty and the Lamb. We do not gain eternal life through our own righteousness, salvation comes only through the righteousness of God. The prophet Isaiah announces: *"I will rejoice greatly in the LORD, my soul will exult in my God; for He has clothed me with garments of* salvation, He has wrapped me with a robe of righteousness." (Isaiah 61:10)

> Blessed are the merciful, for they shall receive mercy.

God has been so merciful to us as sinners. The Apostle Paul calls Him; "*the Father of mercies.*" *(2 Corinthians 1:3)* We have been given the gift of salvation when we didn't deserve it. If we have received such great mercy, shouldn't we be merciful to others? To do so shows gratitude for what we have received and this is pleasing to our heavenly Father. To show mercy shows that we are "*children of God.*" Jesus Himself taught this when He said: "*Be merciful, just as your Father is merciful.*" *(Luke 6:36)*

> Blessed are the pure in heart, for they shall see God.

This speaks of the transformation on the inside. True Christianity is not following a series of rules on the outside, as the Pharisees did, or as many religious people do. It is a complete transformation of the inner man, the real person. God speaking though the prophet Ezekiel said "*I will give you a new heart and put a new spirit within you.*" *(Ezekiel 36:26)* The Apostle Paul said God chose David to be king of Israel because he had a heart for God: "*He raised up David to be their king, concerning whom He also testified and said, 'I have found David the son of Jesse, a man after My heart, who will do all My will.*" *(Acts 13:22)* To have a heart for God means that you are determined to do the will of

God, no matter what the cost. We all long to be pleasing to our heavenly Father.

> *Blessed are the peacemakers, for they shall be called sons of God.*

Our Lord Jesus Christ is a *"peacemaker."* After all, He went to the cross to make peace between God and man. As in everything pertaining to the Christian life, we are to behave like Christ. When we present the gospel we are telling others how they too can have peace with God through Jesus Christ. The Bible teaches us to live in peace with the world around us. I believe that forgiveness is an aspect of this. We can be offended and have conflict with others, or we can forgive and make peace. Speaking of Christ, the Apostle Peter said; *"while being reviled, He did not revile in return; while suffering, He uttered no threats, but kept entrusting Himself to Him who judges righteously."* (1 Peter 2:23)

> *Blessed are those who have been persecuted for the sake of righteousness, for theirs is the kingdom of heaven.*

The unrighteous of this world hate the righteous. They hated Jesus when He was in this world. Once again, when we conduct ourselves like our Lord and Savior, this is a good indication that we are true Christians. The Apostle Paul informs us that; *"all who desire to live godly in Christ Jesus will be persecuted."* (2 Timothy 3:12) The Apostle John tells us to expect hatred from the world: *"Do not be surprised,*

brethren, if the world hates you." (1 John 3:13) The Apostle Paul says that suffering for Christ is our calling: *"For to you it has been granted for Christ's sake, not only to believe in Him, but also to suffer for His sake."* (Philippians 1:29)

> *Blessed are you when people insult you and persecute you, and falsely say all kinds of evil against you because of Me. Rejoice and be glad, for your reward in heaven is great; for in the same way they persecuted the prophets who were before you.* (Matthew 5:3-12)

We have reason to be glad when we are persecuted for our faith in Christ. The true prophets who were sent to Israel were insulted, persecuted, tortured and even killed because they proclaimed the truth of God. The people almost always believed the false prophets, just as many people believe false teachers today. When we are insulted and persecuted because we are Christians, we are to rejoice. This shows that we are in the family of God and not the family of the devil. Christians will always be a minority in this world, because we believe and proclaim the truth of God. Yet through Jesus Christ, we are also victors in this world. Jesus defeated the devil, sin and death and this victory is ours to claim if we are truly born again.

The Apostle Peter gives both warning and encouragement to all who call themselves Christian: *"He has granted to us His precious and magnificent promises, so that by them you may become partakers of the divine nature, having escaped the corruption that is in the world by lust. Now for this very reason also, applying all diligence, in your faith supply moral excellence, and in your moral excellence, knowledge, and in your knowledge, self-control, and in your self-control, perseverance, and in your perseverance, godliness, and in your godliness, brotherly kindness, and in your brotherly kindness, love. For if these qualities are yours and are increasing, they render you neither useless nor unfruitful in the true knowledge of our Lord Jesus Christ. For he who lacks these qualities is blind or short-sighted, having forgotten his purification from his former sins. Therefore, brethren,* **be all the more diligent to make certain about His calling and choosing you.**" *(2 Peter 1:4-10)*

To close this book I would just like to encourage everyone who claims to be Christian to keep examining yourselves. Remember that we are at war and the battles don't end until we leave this world. This war is a spiritual war and we fight with spiritual weapons. We will have successes and failures, but we can rest in the knowledge that our Lord Jesus Christ has already claimed victory over the enemy. We fight the battles, knowing that the war has already been won. My prayer is that the true church will shine forth brightly in this world and present the gospel as our Lord and Savior commanded. It is to His glory that we live. It is to His glory that we are truly born again.

So let me encourage you all:

>   To read and study the Bible.
>   To live a life of obedience to God.
>   To preach the gospel.
>   To worship - worship being an act of giving to God; we give our praise and even ourselves.

To exhort, admonish and encourage the saints.
To love - God, Jesus, Christians and non-believers.
To Pray.
To live by faith and not by sight.
To deny yourself by putting the deeds of the flesh to death.
To live in the Spirit by saturating yourself in the word of God.
To focus on God and His kingdom and not on worldly things.
To live a life of humility - never exalt yourself; remember that everything is a gift from God.
To have a servant attitude - treat others like they are more important than you.
To beware of false teachers - avoid them and expose their teachings to others.

Printed in the USA
CPSIA information can be obtained
at www.ICGtesting.com
CBHW071233100224
4219CB00046BC/1342